The Inflatable Life

The Inflatable Life

Mark Laba

an imprint of Anvil Press

Copyright © 2019 by Mark Laba

All rights reserved. No part of this book may be reproduced by any means without the prior written permission of the publisher, with the exception of brief passages in reviews. Any request for photocopying or any other reprographic copying of any part of this book must be directed in writing to ACCESS: The Canadian Copyright Licensing Agency, One Yonge Street, Suite 800, Toronto, Ontario, Canada M5E 1E5.

"a feed dog book" for Anvil Press

Anvil Press Publishers Inc.
P.O. Box 3008, Station Terminal
Vancouver, BC V6B 3X5
www.anvilpress.com

Imprint editor: Stuart Ross
Cover design: Rayola.com
Interior design & typesetting: Stuart Ross
Illustrations for "Tolstoy's Leech Farm" by the author
feed dog logo: Catrina Longmuir

> Library and Archives Canada Cataloguing in Publication
>
> Title: The inflatable life / Mark Laba.
> Names: Laba, Mark, author.
> Description: Poems.
> Identifiers: Canadiana 20190088702 | ISBN 9781772141429 (softcover)
> Classification: LCC PS8573.A12 I55 2019 | DDC C811/.54—dc23

Printed and bound in Canada

Represented in Canada by Publishers Group Canada
Distributed in Canada by Raincoast Books; in the U.S. by Small Press Distribution (SPD)

The publisher gratefully acknowledges the financial assistance of the Canada Council for the Arts, the Canada Book Fund, and the Province of British Columbia through the B.C. Arts Council and the Book Publishing Tax Credit.

To my wonderful daughter Mia because she was the first to express an interest in having her name in a book. As for Karen, Eli, and Julien, like Don Knotts in The Reluctant Astronaut, *they've shown some trepidation in this outer-space world of poetry, but I'll win them over in the long run, so I'm throwing them in.*

Contents

Phil's Wall Unit Emporium / 9
Prodigal Son Toupée / 12
Boxcar Fred / 14
Tolstoy's Leech Farm / 15
Tennis Lessons for the Homeless / 26
Cold Meat City / 28
German Without Toil / 30
How to Determine the Proper Geometrical Angle for Putting
    One's Nose to the Grindstone / 31
The Wallace Stevens Hit Parade
    Gutterball of Bathsheba / 32
    The Bananas of Dr. Horst / 33
    Four Ways of Looking at an Alligator / 34
    The Emperor of the Ice Cream Truck / 36
The Bratsworthian Elegies by Songmar Oomaplintz
    Norfenlander, translated by Mark Laba / 37
Vomiting into a Grecian Urn / 38
Penticton Haiku / 40
Shaggy Dog Vest Pockets of the Kalahari / 42
The Bruised Sunset / 44
The Mah-Jong Head-Bob / 46
Moonlit Lung Serenade / 47
Smallpox for Dummies / 50
Death by Chop-a-Matic / 54
The Inflatable Life / 55
Toilet Duck / 58
Ordering Online / 59
Killmaster—Arms of Vengeance / 60

Season of the Corn Dog / 65
When a Knuckleball Calls / 68
A Urinary Tract Runs Through It / 69
Television Habits / 70
Dr. Zhivago's Lawn Mower / 71
Taking Rotundas by Storm / 72
Skeet Shooting / 73

Phil's Wall Unit Emporium

Do you like wall units
as much as I do?
For instance, sometimes
when I'm visiting someone's house
I will admire their wall unit
and ask them questions about it.
"Is there anything behind your wall unit?" I might say.
"Any party trays with cheese and deli selections?
Any endangered species, whooping cranes, marmosets,
owls, pygmy goats, baby sturgeon swimming in pickle jars
filled with pond scum? Any Nazi artifacts, a secret staircase
that descends to a Russian gymnasium,
huge stashes of toilet bowl cleanser or
a collection of left-footed shoes
stolen from a bowling alley?"

Occasionally I will provide facts to people
with wall units who I'm visiting, like
"Did you know Edgar Allan Poe wrote a story
about a guy who kills someone and then hides
the body behind his wall unit and people come over
to admire the unit and how much stuff it can hold
—like books and a stereo system and some nice
porcelain vases and commemorative cups or
bass-fishing trophies—not knowing that
a dead body lies just behind this lovely display?"
We look at each other and laugh, uncomfortably,
and I begin to suspect that perhaps

they too have killed someone, maybe an uncle
or aunt or neighbour who broke their
lawn mower and stowed them behind their own wall unit
exactly as Edgar Allan Poe depicted it.

A wall unit asks much from its admirer.
It asks to believe the unbelievable
or to disbelieve all that is visible
because the wall unit by nature
is about invisibility,
even if it takes five heavy-set men
to move that invisibility about
or install it in a room
where it must be custom-fitted around
a fireplace or taxidermy marlin or moose head
that was caught, shot and killed
by a great-uncle on your mother's side
but you don't talk to that side of the family anymore:
something about a gravy boat, or maybe it was
a gravy train or maybe a grave misunderstanding
about your uncle being buried in a shallow grave. His
gravity was felt for generations,
pulling and tugging and at times massaging
family memories, even after the flesh has turned flaccid
and the wall unit's been invaded
by termites and covered in the dust produced
by the subtle coughing that people use
to indicate impolite conversation around
gravy boats and dead people.

Maybe you don't see these things
the same way as me but after all I'm Phil,
of Phil's Wall Unit Emporium,
and I don't joke around when the sight
of a blank wall is as terrifying as
when you were a kid and stared directly
at a solar eclipse without the protection
of a toilet paper tube,
risking blindness and the derision of astronauts
you couldn't see but nonetheless knew
were stomping around up there
stirring up moon dust and microbiological life forms
that would one day hitch a ride on an asteroid
and eventually conquer earth.

The earth is just a big wall unit,
an entertainment hub of love and horror,
a barricade between you and those
you have buried behind the wall
and a big glowing stereo system,
its blinking lights
a distant satellite
relaying music that fades as fast
as a shard of winter light briefly caught
in the deadened eye
of a trophy fish.

Prodigal Son Toupée

I don my prodigal son toupée
and make my way to the penthouse suite
where the air smells of gardenias and liverwurst.
Wallace Stevens wrote a poem about this once
before he took up alligator wrestling
and bricklaying in Tuscany.
Rumour is
he lost his left hand to a gator
but had a fake hand made that
he kept in the second drawer of his office desk
on top of some life insurance policies.
He wore it only for bowling
with his cronies and decorating his
grandchildren's birthday cakes.

"HAPPY BIRTHDAY
GOAT BOY" the cake reads—
a windless night
but still the scent from
the handprints left on staplers
and mouldy plastic flowers
steal you away from the canapés
and lost luggage turning on a carousel in Fiji
even though you're in Saskatchewan
but can still feel your palms
scraping together like palm fronds
speckled with Post-it notes that read,
"Don't forget, you're calling the bingo numbers tonight."

Now I just stand around
like a moon-landing countdown,
breath fading quickly as the time on a parking meter,
words collapsing like a portrait of Bliss Carman
tobogganing, and the ink pot empty,
surrounded by turtles
dreaming of hamburger meat and a flat sea
where darkness is bare-legged and sweating
and the earth below
scrabbling and snuffling
like the big snout of a heartless animal,
stall-fed and murderous
as the carpet-sweeping scars
that criss-cross its pudgy face.

Boxcar Fred

The squirrels bark my name
but it's a name I don't use anymore,
a name from the dust bowl of history,
the same dust bowl my barber uses
to cut my hair
whilst the new moon wheezes
overhead.

Tolstoy's Leech Farm

The monarch was invertebrate
and partly submerged
surrounded by quacks and charlatans
who clutched at food as if they were epidermal scales
on godlike amphibians.
Blood-bearing and bloodless
the narrative laboured
with geographical egg-laying
and makeshift terrorizing.

Rip van Winkle awoke
on a semi-fluid sea of magma
teeth oscillating
between child and savage.

Quicker than you can say porcupine plasma
the elasticity of continents
revealed the imprints of anchovies
that acted as magnets for national hostility.

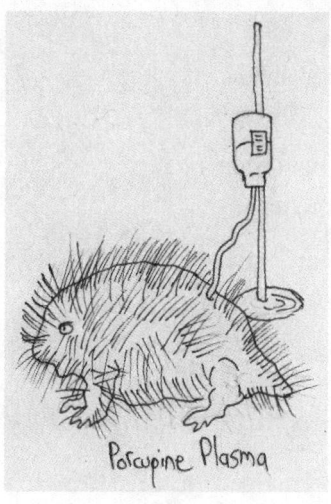

Porcupine Plasma

Lungs gained a foothold
where the woodchuck failed
digging holes
on a farm that grew
spineless toys into bulky vegetarians
clumsy and monosyllabic
grappling with the entrails of a fowl
the task of reconstructing
the fibrils of the tidal machine
the gigantic pistons of memory
churning up carbuncles and beggarly phonetics.

The Woodchuck's Failure

References are absorbed by intestinal walls
and pandered to by the heavy-haired descendants
of guileless farmers
the face, lips and tongues
eager for the moisture
of coupling eulogies.

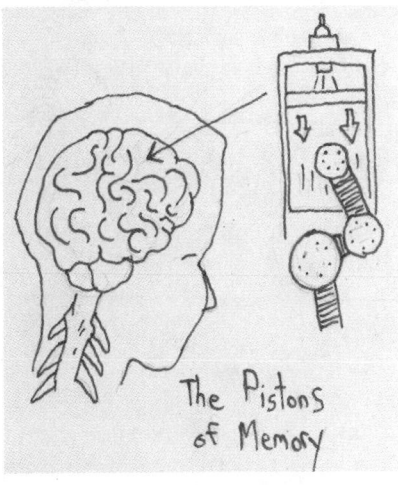

The Pistons of Memory

Proteins resembling paragraphs
enter into the pages
apple pie à la mode
disguised as a yawning chemist.
Coteries of specialized killers
strung together like frogs
converge on sweeping conclusions
with eyeholes for sighting
the swarming alphabet-makers.

A sprained ankle
grows a beard
develops a phraseology
invisible to invading hosts
old-fashioned, radioactive, binary
and waving wands of luncheon fat
against moral lesions.

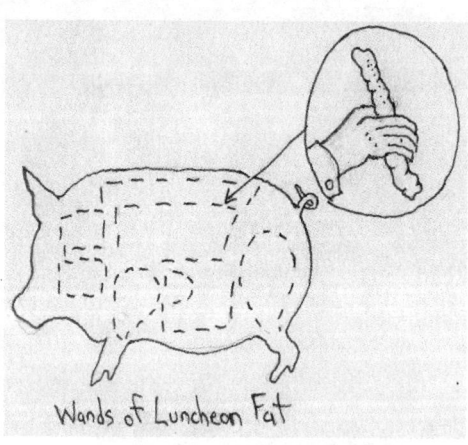

Interpretation becomes a crude picture
allied with pneumatic fictions
kept buoyant with the swing of a battle-axe
spoiling stories with false velocity
even as they shatter
on Herodotus's dental work.

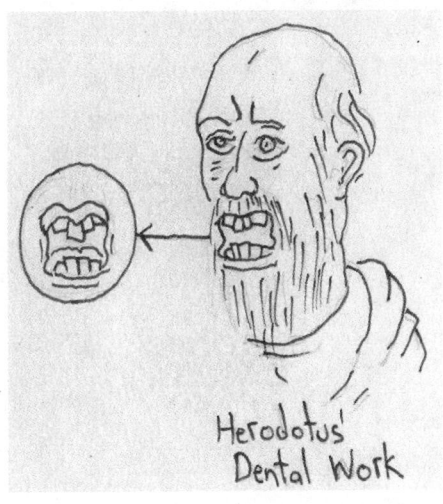

The spying tube
rejects the optic nerve
turns voyages to vapour
and fields full of grandfathers are left
trying to domesticate potato chips
with pugilist blows and virulent poisons.
At the heart of the atomic colony
bachelor protons
search for wives.
Ardent, they rush into the fray

their dialectic blades
their imponderable fluids
bursting into flame.

Domestication of Potato Chips

Doughy champions
like fossil shells
are easily dethroned
shrivelling and shrinking
expatriated appendages
reared in the friction between
dream state and plumbing.

You can't slit a man's throat
without using a three-foot mirror
and whirligigs of fire,
leaving a filmy, tenuous structure
that recalls an infant organism
with nondescript hobbies
and aphid-like flesh

crusty in its ambitions
but causal in its glutinous composition.

Flakes of Poverty

The poet belches insignificantly
the curious and treacherous channels travelled
inevitably lost to ill phrasing
and perishable duplication—
a wax ball that neither sinks nor floats
but hangs somewhere in between—
stationary, stinking of garlic and whisky
but convincing in its atrophied brain
flakes of poverty
icing over the prow of its suffering
and bitter failure shadowing
its recent showing
at the dumbbell competition.

Brazen sanitary feats
of Byzantine flourishes
made previously indecomposable bodies
at ease amongst the furnishings
their internal suction
condensing the familiar arrangements
and excreting a half-million dollars'
worth of mucous membranes
and barbers whose chairs remain empty.

Grasshopper aggression
has led to traversed arcs

suggesting great works of art
germinated by foggy tracery
the eye purging its dross
like a billiard ball refusing to bathe
and abdominal cavities
struggling with the mechanics of
four-limbed commonplace gods
striking at their thistle-flecked progeny.

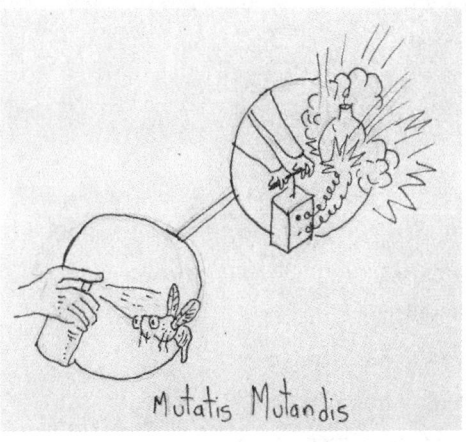

Like the familiar squirrel
but with a longer solidified neck bone
mutatis mutandis
otherwise known as
the stubby-pocketed German cousin
who is always asking, why, why, why
and will wilfully falsify
the disgrace of vain and fabled authors,
be it in the laboratory, factory, drainpipe
or the crater of a volcano.

The Nerve Endings of Shadows

The nerve endings of shadows
are inscribed with something between words
a charred script reflecting
a collision of clouds
or a kidney stone
set against a gorgeous sunset
the earth's interior a muscular action
against a whirling globe.
In leisure moments
we ride from the palaces
into the barriers of progress
sneering, anthologized
spouting steam and coins
as erratic as microbes:
jack-in-the-box geologists
with four-chambered hearts

suckling on the sagging flap of extinction
and the orbit of sluggish suicide
and juggling mice.

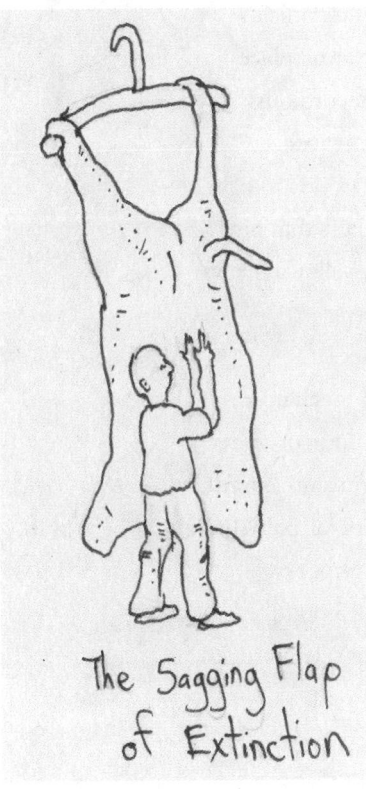

Tennis Lessons for the Homeless

It takes three ingredients
to make a perfect beef stew:
beef, potatoes and jaundice
foraged from a faraway place
where worn-out accordions
wheeze in muddy graves.

Where are the fingers that pine
for those cracked, yellowing keys
fluttering soundlessly
over toothy grimaces
and moss-covered mechanisms
cranking out the music of gnats?
The rheumy eye runs up against
the rough underside of pale sunlight
and a haberdashery peeks
from the depths of a pond
a sign advertising a sale on socks
nearly thirty years past.

I'm not quite as old
as the casket I'm buried in
but it fits me like a glove
and I think I've been putting on weight.
There's no one here anymore
but the incessant pecking
of tiny beaks—
Did I say beaks?

I meant gluten-free loaves of bread
playing whack-a-mole on my head.

I believe in the possibilities of ignorance:
butchers to bankers
bibles to blimps
tennis lessons for the homeless
archaeological digs beneath the kitchen sink.

There's no telling
when the eye's rattling freight
will become as deceitful as a bologna sandwich
resting on a half-finished crossword
abandoned on the seat of a subway train.

I glance down at 32 across.
It wants a word for "Sneeze-guards of Pompeii"
but I'm already ahead of the game
volcanic ash settling on the peak of my baseball cap
and I'm sure the crumpled paper bag
that blows down the empty tunnel
contains the tip of the tongue
upon which that word firmly rests.

Cold Meat City

A shadowy figure
seared my eyeballs
with creamy-crested green waves
while toasted marshmallows
whacked against an oak door.

I felt the throb of gasoline
along my cellophane cigar
and 500 chimneys
squawked defiantly
as I stood like a head of lettuce
impaled on a hand spike
the savage din of cows
tied fast to snowdrifts behind me.

The trees rasped
like dry tongues
and words slipped off
into quarantine
where half-sentences faltered
like soggy firecrackers
and the stone bosom of beauty
fell asleep, a letter opener loose
in her arthritic fist.

Nothing relieved
this twisted voyage of apprehension—
too many false alarms

crackled underfoot
growing into a sharp, evil rhythm
working the street corners like a cafeteria huckster
banging a broken rudder
against the first hints of a thunderstorm.

No camera could capture
this unexpected romance
strung on the scaffolding of tree surgery
and the twitching fingers of perjury
the awkwardness just a notion
a purposeless movement
in search of an audience.

German Without Toil

Das restaurant is pronounced the same as in French
but with a porter shouting, "Hot sausages!"
in the ear of a man loosening his sword
in the smoking compartment.
Later, in the dining car he swallows the sword
and his fellow travellers yell, "But, Mr. Schmidt, you are dead,"
even though he is not, but that's how it is
with sword swallowers in overheated rooms
mourning withered crops, lost wives and the passing of big cigars.

Later his luggage awakes without him in a small town.
It is confused.
The rubbish bin in the lavatory has vanished
and an unassuming young man is teaching a parrot
to swear although neither has shaved for weeks
and they lie beneath the wreckage of charred bodies that
children are told the storks brought. "Please, miss,"
the parrot says, "one liver and one blood sausage
and could you beat them gently with a rubber-soled shoe."

The radio, the home, the coal, the fall, the war.
Be patient, for even if the tailor has disengaged
from the police investigation
there will always be strange stories
and dogs standing out in the rain
licking the back of a drunken man's head
and barking at the huge cheese wheels
changing trains at Münster Hauptbahnhof.

How to Determine the Proper Geometrical Angle for Putting One's Nose to the Grindstone

So soon the fleeting
tasks of youth

remain but the memories fade
like a steamed hot dog shot from the gullet tube

and a newly crowned king bellicose, varicose
warbles at the gates of doom like a wee songbird

greets the day
with a shit, regurgitation and a worm

before retiring to the trampoline park
for a bounce or two.

The Wallace Stevens Hit Parade

Gutterball of Bathsheba

Gutterball, screamed the parakeet;
how often its disgusting little feet
gripped the glint of
morning's false light,
heroics left to the shadows
of naked dwarfs bulging with
the rocking of ramshackle clouds
after the railroad train
pulls out of Peking
and the creamery shutters bang
in the piebald heat.

The Bananas of Dr. Horst

Back at the Waldorf
the world hummed in his handkerchief,
naked tragedy clawing at the tunky-tunky-tunky
planks of bananas, masculine and feminine,
crowded like poodles under parasols.
O Mother, do not enter the foliage
where paratroopers with unhealthy appetites
bear barren fruit of bleak illusion,
and an old man on a mountain is only the remnant anatomy
of tragic puppet spray.
Plinky-plinky-plonk, piano keys of loquacious salad beds—
never were the sounds so unsmelled
than in the labial gardens of Dr. Horst and his bananas,
the arches of Minneapolis fallen
in the savage debris of disillusionment.

Four Ways of Looking at an Alligator

I

A man, a woman and an alligator
wear sagging pantaloons
and smell of summer fields, skeletons and meat gravy,
their shadows traced by blotchy blackbirds with grim hallucination.

II

I was of three minds:
the alligator, the blackbird and a discarded mouth organ
left on the shore of a blobby sea,
dark marine with the hems of beggars' capes,
happy fecundity.
You phantom glass-blowers of North America.

III

Yowzah, yowzah, yowzah
O thin tailors of Vesuvius,
your warbling is the blindness of ground beef,
the inescapable rhythm of newspapers driven by the coughing
that brings poetry to the pineapples of artifice.

IV

Is that an alligator in your pants
or do you just want to rassle me
under the sassafras tree
greased with the jelly of a perplexed machine?
The alligator rests but the blackbird is wary, taciturn.
A papier-mâché ventriloquist dead on a sofa near Lake Geneva
knows this and remains bitter as a dried leaf
pressed between the pages of a nudie book
begetting tubas
and purple prunes of engorgement.

The Emperor of the Ice Cream Truck

Roll out the barrel
and yell hap-hap hallow,
for the wench is but a cataleptic polymathic hierophant vassal
born of Mrs. Papadopoulos.
We all scream ice cream
with gawky beaks
as the emperor rubs himself
with weak facts and an old fantouche,
lacking a personalia and a dog-eared vocabulary.
It's just booming vulgarity
in vanilla or chocolate.
So don't even ask for coconut,
you lewd opiate of chastity and musty teeth.

Affix your fuzzy wig
to your knobby, swollen head
and inhale the odours of the fantails of Oklahoma,
then ask yourself with trembling lip and palaver of hand,
what do you want, a rifle butt or a sugar cone?
Beep, beep,
don't touch my bumper of doom,
you concupiscent curd of a human,
for I am the Emperor of the Ice Cream Truck
and no, I do not
have any pistachio.

The Bratsworthian Elegies by Songmar Oomaplintz Norfenlander, translated by Mark Laba

Odiferous goats of dusk,
clinging dusk,
you penetrate my flinching buttocks,
whooping on beaten hooves riddled with corn husks.
Is this not a trampoline of despair and lost shoes?
Must I jump for hours until someone finds my shoes
and dispenses some aspirin for my bouncing, soulless mood?
Sneeze, sneeze, then spray saliva no more
upon the strudel of doom.

The ventriloquist's underpants
cast a heavy shadow across the porcupine's brow.
But—what's that? The plinking of a dissolute piano string
choking the horse penis of the evening? Yes, yes,
cries the Matzoh Meal Man,
stomp not upon the house of remorseful goat people
or the clomp-clomp of their childless wombs.

My hovering globules of life, o globules of life, do not
forgo the broth of your fecund mind or the ant tunnels beneath.
Even webbed feet must be kissed from time to time
and maybe greased with fluids of ethereal delights.
Still, the shoe inserts may evade your fingers
when night drops its mallet of despair,
but the ants in your toreador pants shall
always be welcome in our house.

Vomiting into a Grecian Urn

On this TV show,
tiny people are wrestling
with a giant telephone.
The same phone that's connected to
the voice inside your head.
It rings.
"Hello," you say.
"Hey," says the voice on the other end.
"There's a commercial coming up I think
you'll really enjoy. It has two-headed umpires and
a lovable puppet that vomits lug nuts into a Grecian urn,
not to mention
a Lazy Susan that descends
like the second coming of Christ,
scattering deli-meat shrapnel
into the foreheads of the unwarned,
the unwanted and the unwary."
"What about the unwashed?" I ask.
"Nah. Nobody wants them. Not even God."

This is one of those moments when
you're in or you're out,
although either way
you'll end up on the outskirts of wherever your head hits
after airing some of your piddling regrets
to the wrong crowd whose collective love
after the loss of their Grecian urn
drives them to murder

and the subsequent disposal of your body
in a nearby pond whose sewage runoff
creates blooms of cancerous beauty
woven into the tendrils of the water lilies
where bullfrogs laze and cry like babies
when you catch them and hold them
upside down by the legs
on a hot summer afternoon.

Penticton Haiku

Forest fire ash
settles like snowflakes
over the Ramada Inn hot tub.

> Statue of a Sasquatch
> in an RV park. A beer can
> clutched in its fibreglass hand.

Ten heads swivel
in a drive-thru fast-food line.
A seagull plucks a fish from a golf-course pond.

> The sound of crickets
> faint beneath the air conditioner's hum
> and *Okanagan Wild Wrestling* on local television.

The pulse of automatic lawn sprinklers
lulls me to sleep. Bats feed on bugs
under the gas station lights.

> Wineries rise
> above industrial parks.
> The grapes of wrath mingle at Canadian Tire.

Shadows of lawn furniture
thrown against the stucco walls of balconies.
A spoiled muffler echoes off sandstone cliffs.

    Yet again I lose a fuzzy prize
    at the claw machine
    in the bus depot.

Ogopogo replicas
litter the landscape
like 7-Eleven sea serpents.

    A container of dew worms
    and a Big Gulp
    nestled in the minivan's cupholders.

The sound of the lake
at night, punctuated
by the squeak of inflatable toys.

Shaggy Dog Vest Pockets of the Kalahari

Two grouse hunters
were searching for cigarettes in my dream
when they stepped in a suspicious puddle
that jerked on their veins. I awoke to find
the president nearby; he put down his
binoculars and cried, "I just saw a big alligator
dancing with an X-ray specialist, and a
knife-thrower with shell-pink ears planting rhubarb
on the complaint manager's grave."
All fine and dandy but still I wondered
why the pedestrians got all dolled-up
just to be run over by a parking lot attendant
who was getting hoity-toity with a corn-husking coroner
over a marble-topped chicken coop.
You'd need to bring a wheelbarrow
to an afternoon cocktail party to understand
you were jumping from 20,000 feet without a parachute,
but a priest, a rabbi and a bag of fertilizer add
to the joke's weight, plus a hangover that spoke
in eleven languages but could still warble
like a Pentagon general abandoned in the Sahara
with only a windshield-wiper blade to ward off
smallpox, syphilis and the fake beards of horse thieves.
You can tie a yacht to a dock
but you can't make it drink nor can you entice
a Scandinavian servant to sob over your typewriter keys.
Juggle it all with six cents to a mile
and a goat in a magnolia bush

milking million-dollar deals from gangsters in the shrubbery
and you've got a little hocus-pocus in the bathtub
and Shakespeare in the midst of an earthquake
wearing a short skirt and plagiarizing raccoons
before a sobbing magistrate.

> *"Sign of the times,"*
> *said the suidical termite,*
> *"and whether you smoke, drink*
> *or gamble, you'll always find Plato*
> *with a can of lima beans*
> *between his knees, pressuring*
> *honeymooners to scoff*
> *at stockholders mooching dandruff paste*
> *from coconut-maraca magnates."*

The Bruised Sunset

The sunset
is the same hue
as the bruise
Martin Xavier gave me
in Grade 6
when he punched me
in the face
after I suggested
he was a schmuck.
Such is the power of suggestion
and the power of a sunset
in the distorted face
of a recollected youth,
a pain that reaches across years
stinging like a jellyfish,
inadvertent, unseen, undulating on the
murky waters of memory, blind
and muddied with shame.

My shame and not the jellyfish's
because after all it's just jelly
and pulsating sacs and feeding tubes,
and me, well, suffice to say
my knees were jelly
and I could only wish
back then
for the tentacles of death
to strike back

at every water-fountain foe
and gravel-dusted playground enemy
while I sought solace
up in a tree,
one eye tracing airplane vapour trails
and bugs navigating tree bark
while with the other
I watched Martin Xavier
beat up my friend beneath the tree.
When he asked if I wanted to switch places
after I voiced my concern,
I just grinned sheepishly.
All these years later
I'm still up in that tree,
cowardly, trembling,
always willing to sacrifice someone else
so I can continue to enjoy the rustling leaves,
the purity of poetry
and the smell of overdone barbecued pork
wafting on the breeze.

The Mah-Jong Head-Bob

A sinister warning
carried on the wings of a hesitant budgie.
"Capitalist pig," it chirped.
"You said it, toots,"
I replied, beating my face like
exfoliated meat on
the typewriter keys.
What was it to be?
A speechless couple ready to punch my ticket?
A photo of Orson Welles in his underpants plucking a chicken?
A cravat with cigar burns, lying on the side of a desert highway?
All I know is that if you weighed my despair
it would be about half a pound of flank steak.

There's murder in the air,
darkening my breakfast nook
where I eat Cap'n Crunch and stare down the budgie.
"You shoulda been a crow," I say between mouthfuls.
"You shoulda been Hans Christian Andersen dying
of mushroom poisoning," the budgie replied.

I look out the window.
The sky is a giant pinball machine.
Nobody has any business being here,
especially me, but then again,
if I were a one-armed xylophone player from Baltimore
it would be a whole different story.

Moonlit Lung Serenade

I was sitting on the bus singing to myself, not too loudly
but apparently loud enough because I was singing
Neil Young's "Cinnamon Man,"
the one that goes,
"I want to live with a cinnamon man,
I could be happy with a cinnamon man.
A dreamer of pictures
a stick for your coffee,
glowing in the moonlight
sweetening your drink.
Send me some money
because cinnamon man isn't cheap
and he has to pay for his dry cleaning
every time he dunks in your coffee.
Cinnamon man, mmmmmm, mmmmmm,
cinnamon man, uh huh,
cinnamon man…"
and then the guy next to me said, "Jesus, you fucking retard, it's cinnamon girl, not cinnamon man," but I wasn't startled by his calling me this, as my mother used this same name for me too but only on special occasions like at Christmas or during miniature golf outings when she'd yell, "Jesus Christ, you fucking retard, you gotta get the ball between the windmill blades," while she fished around for the mickey of rye she had stuffed down the crotch of her hot pants, but what startled me was this cinnamon man/girl thing. All these years I'd pictured this happy cinnamon stick with a top hat and little arms and legs dancing across tabletops, not unlike Mr. Peanut but minus

the monocle and spats, twirling a cane perhaps before diving headfirst into a nice steaming cup of coffee, and now I find out I had it all wrong? Well, number one, I lost all respect for Neil Young after that and then everything got real blurry and then the bus crashed and when I woke up I was covered in body parts and giant rock pipit feathers. How do I know they were rock pipit feathers? Well, the rock pipit's plumage is darker than the meadow pipit's, which has a more muted, speckled, streaked colouring and is also known for its piping cry rather than the rock pipit's more guttural and, some say, regurgitative-sounding song. In Sardinia and Iceland they are eaten with a bit of grainy mustard and washed down with vodka and bidet water. Anyway, judging by the size of these feathers, no one would be eating this rock pipit any time soon and, sure enough, as I crawled from the bus wreckage, a rock pipit the size of a Napoleonic War statue was standing behind me pecking at passersby and lopping off their heads as easily as if they were Q-tips. I've never handled a gun before but I pretended I had one and I pointed it at the rock pipit and called up to its inquisitive giant head, "What do you want with us and why did you do that to the bus?" The rock pipit considered me for a moment, a cocked shining beady eye reflecting back my own tear- and blood-streaked face and body, and lo and behold I'll be damned if I didn't see in that giant rock pipit eye my own colourful and beautiful plumage rustling in the breeze and the heat from the bus that had now caught fire, while inside, anyone still alive was screaming for mercy. The rock pipit opened its beak and out dropped a cinnamon stick and above the noise of fire and carnage the rock pipit let out its great regurgitative cry, and I put down my imaginary gun and bent to wash my hands in a cool blue pool of bus antifreeze. It's a terrible thing, jealousy, whether it's plumage or trying to steer your Buick while battling dual personalities like Odysseus returning home to find the lights off and all the locks changed, moonlight flecking a darkened sea like flashes of memory or golf balls striking against aluminum siding and the shadows of miniature windmill blades slicing the still air as if beheading the unseen.

Smallpox for Dummies

The only cure for smallpox
(that I know of)
besides looking at old photos of
smallpox victims
is to go to your local library
and estimate every square foot of concrete
leading up to the building
by using shoeboxes
worn over your feet.
It takes a few days of shuffling but
you'll get used to it. I did.
So did the president of the United States.
We shuffled together for a while but then
he had to go away
in a helicopter
to drop Hummel figurines
on some children
in a hot-tub manufacturing plant
at the edge of a planet he had
recently declared flat.
We did have a nice conversation about
chicken wings and
the proper diameter and spacing
of the dowelling
for poultry cages.

Don't buy it? Look down
at your own feet

and tell me if you don't believe
what your feet have seen
and remind you of every night
as you have recurring dreams of
walking across a vast desert
speckled with dead benefactors
that you once mistook for stars or
an irreversible fungus growth
its spores carried on a gutless wind
torn from the valley's throat
and the promise of a rent-free storage facility
for your shadowy pursuits.

Anyway, that was another life
and a melodramatic way of saying
I'd be a monkey's uncle
if I cared but I'm really
a cousin, twice-removed
so it doesn't count
at least under the porch light and a spring rain
that smells like a vegetable platter
leftover from a cocktail party gone wrong
before the galoshes could be sorted out
and people sent wandering
into the serial-killer night.

Schmaltz hearing?

You heard right. I heard wrong.
The last time I had my hearing checked
was when the herring were running.

I've been running all my life
but unlike herring I have feet
although I'm not sure what
I've been running from
but I have some thoughts.
Fish?
Fat?
Proteins?
Doorstoppers?
Doppelgängers?
Corroded batteries in a toy that
sleepwalks on padded feet?

So now I dream I'm sleepwalking
exploring kitchen drawers and
TV remotes
while someone on a couch stares in fear
and skin flakes rain down
like pixels on a failing
computer screen
gathering on the broadloom
like a first snowfall in Vermont
not far from where Robert Frost
had diarrhea beneath the very tree
where he lost in pinochle
only a year earlier

to an acorn-clutching rodent
suffering the stress of hibernation
and a lack of nourishment.

As far as I'm concerned
that fork in the road went to
Squirrel Town every time
and you can shape it like a stigmatism but
everyone knows a rodent-schtupper
when they see one
especially on a snowy evening
with the plumes of horse's breath
swirling and fogging the frantic pacing
of this final frosting
and winter's nuts buried
like nuclear fallout shelters from the '50s
in the backyard
next to the family dog.

Death by Chop-a-Matic

I like television.
It offers a welcome relief
from the hardscrabble dreams
where I work for a living.
What with the basketballs,
parasitic twins and
Cornish game hens
it's a wonder anyone has any time for weaning
the carnivorous offspring of
lumber barons
from the teat of
crappy loon calls
throughout history.

The Inflatable Life

If you line everything up just right
you can probably see the moon
from your grave or from the waves
where the dead stop to blow up
their inflatable toys.
If you're not dead, well
that's a whole other story.
Then you need to begin with
a compass, a shovel and
a cloud shaped like
Franklin Delano Roosevelt's pince-nez
balanced on the snout of
a foraging armadillo
plus a tranquilizer gun
to complete the job
and put to bed
all those bedridden thoughts
you have to turn over
from time to time
to avoid the trigger-finger anticipation
you court with the twitching mayhem
of uneasy brickwork
and colicky peacocks
spreading their feathers
like soft butter on glass.

Is this just another
crappy portage of imagery

slogging it over broken pine cones and
cracked Slushie cups
to finally arrive at a hidden lake
where the trout leap like slot machines set free
from the sweaty grips of pensioners, their
sagging earlobes swelling with
heart-attack juice and the resilient
cartilage of their forefathers
who ground wheat into dust using only
their dentures and copies of
Reader's Digest
stained with grasshopper blood
or is this simply a chance encounter
with your doppelgänger
at an outlet mall where
you both reach for the same bath mat
the last one left in blue and
as your eyes meet
you finally sense
you were not who you thought yourself to be
even when you were thinking about yourself
as someone else who was thinking
of themselves as you?

This is a common complaint
heard from those in the
bath-mat industry and also
the unwitting doppelgängers
caught like deer in headlights
of a purchasing rage

a day built of mirrors and
money and mutton chops
cooling on the windowsill
not to mention the lineups at
the makeshift confessional
where a mind-reading hubcap
discovered in the back of a tool shed
holds court over the muddled brows
pressed to the shiny dented metal
reflecting the unpromised mileage
you think you'll get if you can
just keep your foot off the brake
long enough to
get to hell.

Toilet Duck

I belch
like my father but
his father didn't belch like
anyone I know of
but then again
I wasn't alive then
so who the hell belched like who
I really couldn't tell you
except for the fact
that my digestive tract
stretches back
to Russia in 1908
and I've been passing gas and pogroms
ever since.
Let me tell you
that ain't no picnic
even if you're at a picnic
and I've been to plenty
let me tell you
they ain't no picnic.

Ordering Online

The chiropodist is pensive
around the butterflies
though they're pinned
to old brocade
sending dust motes spinning
like the stuttering signals
of abandoned TV shows
and reports of wars that ended
around the time my
mother's friend Cookie lost her mind
and ordered Chinese takeout
for the entire Russian army
that she envisioned sleeping
in her neighbour's backyard.

Killmaster—Arms of Vengeance

I

Clawing at the edge of the futon
like an open-mouthed plutonium bomb
pumping dust and dirt spurt
from girded loins
while the brunette raised the blowgun
aiming at the bloody and backward
spiritual rebirth
egg-shaped and cradling
a small blindfolded dog.
The arms of vengeance
are rarely mollified
whether it be over breakfast
or under the long stares of bookkeepers
and you can take the bit between the teeth
or a bullet in the loose language of memory
but the topper is a patched-up apology
in a secret embassy with
a bunch of sagging assassins
undoing their bolo ties and
relinquishing their disguises
in order to return
to a furnished room
where the rent is never due.

II

Ambushed by wildflowers
amongst the American industrial imagination
a feeble ripple that showed off the
athletic muscles and full breasts
of Soviet stubbornness
slick with headache lint
and after-dinner activities
a gigantic ramshackle ant's nest
now a training camp for alien ambition
and grimaces on the forest's belly.

Hidden equipment
yawned with fatigue
tired of the fierce eyes and foul cigars
chomping at antiquated honcho smocks.
The Killmaster hissed toilet steam
slipping into the limping ruins
of Paraguay's trap door
lizard-skinned and tougher
than a six-armed error
wearing a powder-blue tuxedo and
throwing mammoth rubble
into the nuclear reactor.

III

The half-starved streets of history
jabbered about sidewalks and taxes
and invisible gleaming shrubbery
the stink of bloody verandas
strangling the sword of god
like lush vegetation around
the sickening echo
of tactical weaponry
in relation to overstuffed furniture
showered with blood from a bum-footed
Mexican standoff gone wrong.

IV

The booby-trapped butler
walked into the oligarch's ambush
monkey-suited and
curated by interoffice snobbery.
Vague shapes unlatched themselves
from radioactive glory
with nose-stinging carnage
the shock sudden
but the destruction as laquered
as the peeled-off socks of
double-crossing and dirty-joke-telling
downhill bicycle throngs
their knells of doom
swelling like pants gas as they
infiltrated the breeder reactor room
behind the local pub.

V

With one gulp
of wooden animal hair
oak turning into pines
turning into patio groins
beeping at the consoles of
nervous neighbours
and uneasy agents
flooding through the corridors
love and violence
close behind
vengeance is mine
or it could've been if I hadn't been hallucinating
about Hitler's hips swaying to the twenty-first century
while an antiquated population
took to hand-sewing manuscripts
and the hot cobblestones
reeked of defecation
and spent AK-47 casings
not to mention confused poultry
tapping out tunes with their beaks
that could make sailors weep
should they ever reach shore.

Season of the Corn Dog

Trotsky was schtupping
Winnie-the-Pooh
at Land O' Lakes
Rifle Range & Petting Zoo
putting me completely off my corn dog
and making me miss
the tractor pull.
Next thing I knew
I was pissing razor blades
in a makeshift urinal
fashioned from a watermelon,
the shadows of dirigibles
passing overhead.

Puts a man in mind of
World War II,
this sense of belonging
to a community
of crustaceans
living beneath the rubble
and all that ballyhoo
when Poland went tits up
and black-market cheese
was made from cigarette butts.

History is written
by those with pincers
and succulent flesh humming

beneath a carapace fashioned from
pipe cleaners and the grim reminders
of the many washed overboard
when nematodes
controlled the earth.

Moreover, kung fu is no match
for Rutger Hauer birthing worms
out back of a glass-eye fabrication plant,
his face like grizzled sirloin
even in the cool air rising
from the nearby ravine,
stacks of rubber tires
hidden by lush ferns that
smell like rain-dampened shoelaces.

There are ears of corn
and walls with ears
listening uneasily
for the easy answer
in a city where parades loom
like distant thunder.
Words bubble and spit on the pavement,
not unlike that 1940s musical
where Jimmy Durante gets gunned down
by the orphans of the Midwest,
their eyes saucers of milk
half-lapped by mewling and mangy cats
whose progeny would later become
YouTube hits.

"I'm sorry, sir,"
security tells me,
"but there's no carrion allowed
in your carry-on."

Well,
that sealed the deal,
put the nail in the coffin
and me coughing
from spores of pollen floating,
talk about regeneration, I'm talking
calypso shuffleboard on a sinking cruise ship,
Bermuda shorts crusted with barnacles and half-used Band-Aids
and a band half-heartedly sawing away
on recalcitrant violins.

You can put that extra buffet plate away
and head for the showers.
Losing is for the young,
but broken compasses and bloodied lobster bibs
are for the brave.

When a Knuckleball Calls

Baseball is for the birds
and by that I mean
there is a bird of some species
chattering incessantly
while I nod off in the bleachers
the last of the sun's rays
speckling me like a skin disease
but the possibilities
are winking in
a faulty scoreboard and
short-circuited wiring
smoking like a burnt hot dog
in the ninth inning
of a little league game
my son on third and, by the looks of it
never coming home
at least not that summer.

A Urinary Tract Runs Through It

The blood is
its own raging ocean
fed by too many rivers
and too few tributaries
with great blue herons
on the shoreline
plucking at rusted watches
and fat deposits,
their long beaks sending
cog wheels and springs
pinging off globs of seaweed
as if table tennis
were a pastoral game
and not an exercise
in sweat and veins.

Television Habits

Liturgical surgical dirigible
singing like the last mutton-hooped
route to the big house
where my father is serving time
for invasive worm species.
Hasn't stopped me from
robbing demarcation zones
and playing plutocrat with
oven mitts and a faulty microwave.
Don't get all high up on your nocturnes
or your ocular rejoicements for nigh
I am Crooked House Man,
last in the line of
my crooked family,
recently OD'd on Lipozene
while astride a Lipizzaner horse
that held the weight on my shoulders
the way trapeze artists hold gravity
in their sweaty palms,
my eyes like puckered tacos
perched on the marble countertop
of a new condo showroom
about to become
a murder scene.

Dr. Zhivago's Lawn Mower

The light is different here.
It ricochets rather than
reflects and objects stab the eye,
causing tear ducts to crumple up
like balls of paper in a wastebasket
waiting for the janitor
who will never arrive
since he hanged himself in the broom closet
next to a dried salami and
a map of the Ottoman Empire
with mustard smudges next to the good parts.

Taking Rotundas by Storm

I saw a man with no ear, he was in the supermarket buying soup and beer and rutabagas from Hungary but I wasn't hungry and I could see inside his head a place like a tree fort where I once played as a kid escaping the heat of a summer's day that was heating up the century like a vat of bubbling cheese or a bunch of dirty magazines with Tater Tot rot beneath the skin's bark and a starling screeching for dumpster space.

Skeet Shooting

I put some language in a bag
and shook it up with crushed bread crumbs.
Boy, the kids like that for dinner but you've got to use melted
butter or the crumbs won't stick to the words.
You can also use crushed potato chips to add variety
and it helps if you speak in tongues during the process
and when I say speak in tongues I mean
you actually have to push the words up through your taste buds
which will create shimmering globules of letters,
incandescent, slimy and completely without meaning.
Some won't even form words at all, just
grunts and sighs and belches.
Rinse them well for there may be toxins
and then arrange them in such a way
that they are easily accessible for
the skeet-shooting machine.
Because, after all, this isn't poetry,
it's a shooting gallery.

Acknowledgements

Some of these poems appeared in slightly different versions previously:

"Tusk-a-Loose'a" as a chapbook by Puddles of Sky Press (Kingston, 2017).

"Prodigal Son Toupée" in *The Northern Testicle Review* #1 (Cobourg, 2016).

"Shaggy Dog Vest Pockets of the Kalahari" in *Matrix* 103 (Montreal, 2015).

"Four Ways of Looking at an Alligator" from "The Wallace Stevens Hit Parade" in *Hava LeHaba* (Tel Aviv, 2014).

"The Mah-Jong Head-Bob" on *The Week Shall Inherit The Verse* (online, 2012).

Mark Laba is a writer and artist living in Vancouver. He cut his teeth in the early-'80s Toronto small press scene before hightailing out to the West Coast. His early published work is ephemeral in nature, taking the form of leaflets and the odd chapbook. His first poetry chapbook, *Movies in the Insect Temple* (Proper Tales Press), appeared in 1981. In 1985, his chapbook *The Mack Bolan Poems* (Gesture Press) won the first bpNichol Chapbook Award. After a long hiatus, *Dummy Spit* (Mercury Press, 2002) was published, and Mark again went into hiding, emerging now and again to be included in the anthology *Surreal Estate: 13 Canadian Poets Under the Influence* (The Mercury Press, 2005) and Stuart Ross's collection of collaborative poems, *Our Days in Vaudeville* (Mansfield Press, 2013). His most recent chapbook, *Tusk-a-loose'a* (Puddles of Sky Press), appeared in 2017. Mark has a long, storied career as a jackass-of-all-trades, working as a watchmaker, anatomical model painter, name-tag maker, faux finisher for artists' wall tiles, stock and bond messenger, vertical-blind assembler, darkroom technician, and scriptwriter for animated films on how to deal with conflicts in the business workplace, a topic about which he was ill-equipped to give advice. But he forged on and in 2000 talked his way into being the restaurant reviewer for the Vancouver *Province*, where his column, Mark Laba's Adventures in Dining, ran until 2009. He disappeared after that.

IF YOU ENJOYED THIS FINE MARK LABA BOOK, DON'T MISS:

Parasitic Activity in Sheep of the Lesser Andes

Featuring:

Esophageal High-Resolution Pentagon Attack in Pistachio Magenta
Waves of Sportsfiskerforening
Reagan's Shawarma Surgery
We Breken Thy Hestes With Mangy Real Estate
Slowpoke Bandage Rumours
Nursing Home Mannequin Scarf
Love World Fanny Pack in the USA
Smile Live Soldiers and Other Fuel Consumption Issues
Python Face and the Curvaceous Unemployed Brunette
Dominus Regis Sex Cohort in Hexidecimal Conversion
Asleep With Country Engagement Dreams and Lab Animal Pie-Tasting
Death from Violent Ums
Sour Marxist Noise Theory in Manitoba
Lumber Mill Druids
Le Chemin Tubers avec 2 Bedroom Brie Rancher
Immunogenic Proteins in the Chinchilla News Processing Chain
Relating to the Symbol and Spirit of Idiots in One Place
No Fan of Fluffy Coconuts
Hydrology, Geomorphology and the Fantasy Rowing League
Library of Babel Support

Other Feed Dog Books from Anvil Press

"A Feed Dog Book" is an imprint of Anvil Press edited by Stuart Ross and dedicated to contemporary poetry under the influence of surrealism. We are particularly interested in seeing such manuscripts from members of diverse and marginalized communities. Write Stuart at razovsky@gmail.com.

The Least You Can Do Is Be Magnificent:
New & Selected Writings of Steve Venright
by Steve Venright,
compiled and with an afterword by Alessandro Porco
(2017)

I Heard Something
by Jaime Forsythe
(2018)

On the Count of None
by Allison Chisholm
(2018)

an imprint of Anvil Press